I WILL LIE DOWN THIS NIGHT

I WILL LIE DOWN THIS NIGHT

Melissa Musick Nussbaum

Art by Linda Ekstrom

LITURGY TRAINING PUBLICATIONS

This book was designed by Jill Smith. Gabe Huck was the editor and Deborah Bogaert was the production editor. Typesetting was by Jim Mellody-Pizzato, in Goudy. The book was printed and bound by Quebecor Printing Book Group.

Library of Congress Cataloging-in-Publication Data

Nussbaum, Melissa Musick.
    I will lie down this night / Melissa Musick Nussbaum; art by
  Linda Ekstrom.
        p. cm.
      1. Compline. 2. Divine office. 3. Payer—Catholic Church.
  4. Sleep—Religious aspects—Christianity. I. Title.
  BX2000.68.N87 1995
  265'.1—dc20   95-11973
                                              CIP

ISBN 1-56854-085-X
NPRAY

CONTENTS

To Martin, and to our children

Take my hands, and bless them,
As they bless what they love,
    And long to keep.

FOREWORD

I learned during the year I wrote my Ph.D. dissertation that bedtime reading of a text which I'd be working on the morrow was an almost surefire method of getting a quick start on the next morning's writing. Whatever is on our minds and hearts as we drift into sleep more often than not greets us with the sunrise. Monastic discipline ritualized this truth in the daily chanting of Compline or Night Prayer, after which no word was spoken until the "Lord, open my lips" of Vigils. The Great Silence stretched from the prayer for protection through the night to the call to praise before dawn.

The last words many of us hear before sleep come from a television, and we are awakened by the radio with its music or news. Our time of unconsciousness stretches from the last word on the scandal to the first word on disasters in the making.

Praying into the mystery of the night will not make our streets safer, nor will Night Prayer remove the anxiety of waking to another day without employment. But whether prayed in the solitude of one's bedroom or in the parish hall, with a child drifting off to sleep or with a religious community, Night Prayer can bring the heart back to the source and end of all life, the faithful God whose promise is to be with us in laughter and in tears, in security and in restless questioning.

I Will Lie Down This Night offers liturgical catechesis, accessible resources for prayer and a mystagogy for standing watch through the night (Psalm 134). The rituals of monks and nuns are as far from most of us as is the experience of living in dwellings without electric light and central heating. But the night remains, and, for those who are listening to the inner voice, there is still the whisper of uncertainty and the cry for protection which comes with the onset of deep darkness and silence.

Newcomers to Night Prayer and those who have never stood in the blackness of a Trappist choir while the brothers sang the whole of Night Prayer from memory may want to read the chapters of this work as their first celebration of this prayer. Those who have been praying this hour for years may want from time to time to come early to the place where they will pray and there read a section of this work. The chapter on Night Prayer can serve as fruitful material for *lectio divina* or as reading in preparation for small group study and discussion of the psalms. The stories recounted serve as primers for the pump of our memories of bedtime. The prayers can serve as blessing and balm for those recollections.

Night is to Night Prayer what bread and wine are to the Eucharist. Night is the good gift of creation to which the word of God comes to create a sacrament. May this prayer help to usher us into the sleep of the just that our days might be shaped by God's peace.

Andrew D. Ciferni, OPRAEM.

CHAPTER 1

TELL ME A STORY

I am lying down tonight with God,
and God tonight will lie down with me.

—from the Celtic tradition

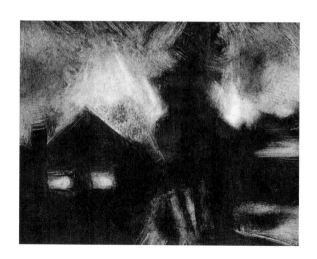

It is the rare household where members improvise bedtime, moving from one bed to another, sleeping this night on the couch and another on a child's bottom bunk. Most of us not only have a bed, "my bed," but we have a preferred side in bed, a particular position in which sleep is most likely to come, even a definite opinion as to the necessary nocturnal arrangements of blankets and pillows. Few adults can sleep until they have reassured themselves that the doors and windows are, indeed, locked and the thermostat is turned down, the alarm is set and the handle on the gurgling toilet has been jiggled. Few children can sleep until they have heard a story and a lullaby and have found the doll or stuffed animal or scrap of worn baby blanket that nightly accompanies them to sleep.

It is possible to sleep without hearing all three verses to "Birmingham Jail." It is possible to lie down and sleep without getting up for a second inspection tour of every door and window. What is not possible is to go to sleep without some kind of ordering of ourselves for the transition from consciousness to unconsciousness, from doing to being, from motion to stillness. It is necessary, in some manner, to put our affairs in order, a foreshadowing of that which we who have sufficient warning will do before our final

descent into sleep and death. The reality is that sleep, like death, is
a journey to a distant country, and we must somehow prepare ourselves for the trip.

Newborn babies are often said to have "their days and nights mixed up." They have no built-in sense of the purposes of day and night, of light and dark. To sleep at all, a baby must often be rocked or walked, and even then will have periods of crying and fussing before finally falling asleep. Gradually, during the second month of life, the baby begins to find ways to settle himself to sleep, to quiet himself from crying. The baby discovers fingers to suck or a mobile to concentrate on. As the months go by, sleep-starved parents listen gratefully in the night for the sounds of an awakened baby first crying, then calming herself as she completes those tasks—finding the fingers, the blanket, the plush toy—which will enable her, quite literally, to settle down for sleep.

Curiously, pediatric researchers write, the newborn who fusses before sleep rests better and sleeps more soundly than the newborn who does not. Small comfort for weary parents, but babies seem to be born with a need to arrange themselves for the transition from wakefulness to sleep: first by fussing, then by patterns of their own devising. As the child grows, the need for a bedtime order remains. Indeed, the first suggestion pediatrician Richard Ferber makes in his book, *Solve Your Child's Sleep Problems*, is to establish a nightly routine of time and place, of word and song, upon which the child can root her own internal arrangements for sleep. And woe unto the parent who misplaces or omits a piece of the ritual. Any blanket, any doll, any song, any story will not do: It must be the familiar companion of many nights, the familiar words which bridge the worlds of light and darkness.

Our son, Andrew, expects to hear "Birmingham Jail" sung at bedtime, but "Birmingham Jail" with a twist: Where the lyrics say "Angels in heaven know I love you," we substitute the name "Andrew" for the word "you." Sometimes I forget to make the change and a small voice, sliding reluctantly into sleep, will remind me, "Say 'Andrew,' Mama. Say my name."

It is a matter of familiarity, of memory, of one of our few remaining connections to oral tradition. For bedtime rituals are the stuff of darkness and lights out, touching hands and faces we can no longer see, speaking words we cannot read, and so must remember.

My husband rolls over "on the wrong side," his face toward me, and I remind him that I cannot go to sleep in that position. My front to his back, cupped like spoons in a drawer, that is how I fall asleep. He protests good-naturedly, then turns to "the right side." I slip my arm around his chest and settle my body against his: familiar and right, ready for sleep.

Our daughter, Anna Kate, long ago outgrew the *Madeline* picture books by Ludwig Bemelmans. But some lines of his caught in our night nets and became part of their fabric:

> *"Good-night, little girl,*
> *Thank the Lord you are well,*
> *And now, go to sleep," said Miss Clavell.*

If I pause, Anna will complete the refrain:

> *And she turned out the light,*
> *And closed the door,*
> *And that's all there is,*
> *There isn't any more.*

If I see a too-late light shining from beneath one of the older children's doors, I will knock and suggest that 6:00 AM will arrive soon, that they should turn out the lights and get some sleep. "I know," comes Betsy's weary answer, "but I can't get to sleep without reading first."

There is a wisdom in our bodies which the church in night prayer recognizes and honors; it is the need for an orderly transition from light to dark, from wakefulness to sleep.

I do not mean to suggest that placing a pitcher of water on the nightstand is night prayer. Placing a pitcher of water on the nightstand every night is part of a pattern, borne out of a human need to order oneself for sleep, and it is as good a place as any to begin. We can recognize that reality and recognize further that, as believers, there is a way to honor our need in words and gestures which address directly the circumstances we face each night: the loss of control, the vulnerability, the "little death" that is sleep.

The church in night prayer respects the hour and those who keep it. Because it is dark during the moments before sleep, the prayers are meant to be prayed in the dark. That is, they change very little from season to season so that the one who prays can rely on memory for the familiar refrains. The church takes what we already know, what we already do, and builds upon that human foundation. Night prayer, or what the church calls "compline," hangs upon a hinge that was in place long before the foundation of the church. We lie down each night. The church reminds us and invites us to celebrate the glad truth that God lies down with us.

I am lying down tonight as beseems
in the fellowship of Christ, Son of the
    Virgin of ringlets,
in the fellowship of the gracious Father of glory,
in the fellowship of the Spirit of powerful aid.

I am lying down tonight with God,
and God tonight will lie down with me,

I will not lie down tonight with sin,
nor shall sin nor sin's shadow lie down with me.

I am lying down tonight with the
    Holy Spirit
and the Holy Spirit this night will lie down
    with me,

I will lie down this night with the Three of
    my love,
and the Three of my love will lie down
    with me.

—from the Celtic tradition

CHAPTER

SING ME A SLEEP SONG

Three things are of God, and these
    three are what Mary told to her
    son, for she heard them in heaven:
The merciful word,
The singing word,
And the good word.

—from the Celtic tradition

The cars of my childhood were like boats, in which we sailed the long, empty roads of west Texas. Unhampered by seat belts, we children draped ourselves over the "hump" on the floor of the back seat, teasing the electric window controls with our bare toes and risking our father's wrath if we sent the glass down far enough to fill the car with the hot, flying sand churned up from the panhandle highways.

Behind the back seat of my father's sedan, a shelf stretched out, abutting the rear window. My aunt stored boxes of tissue and a crocheted "granny afghan" on her shelf; other people adorned them with ceramic dogs, the heads of which were mounted on loose springs so that they bobbled with each pothole and bump in the pavement. But in my father's car, the rear shelf was the place I lay on night trips to watch the stars. It was a happy arrangement: The other children had more room, and I, the youngest child, was occupied with the blanket of stars shaken out and unrolled over my head.

It would get quiet in the car then, as the darkness sealed us inside. There would be no more stops for sodas or stretching or seeing the sights. My father's driving became purposeful. In the night, one races toward a destination, toward light and shelter, toward safety. The night was wild on those country roads, where, even in my childhood, an occasional coyote's cry could be heard. And always in the dark, against the dark, someone would begin to sing. We weren't accomplished enough for harmony, though my sister could manage the alto part on a few Christmas carols, and our repertoire was, as it should have been, limited. Rushing through the darkness toward home, we were bound by memory, bound to the words which we knew by heart. We sang hymns mostly, though my father sometimes would request "Bye Bye Blackbird" or "My Buddy" or "'Til We Meet Again." There was no particular order: Someone would begin singing the melody and the rest of us would follow. We could do that because we knew them all, the songs that we sang on those trips, the rhythms which rolled with us down vapor-lit roads toward home:

Abide with me, fast falls the eventide.
The darkness deepens: Lord, with me abide.
When other helpers fail and comforts flee,
Help of the helpless—O, abide with me.

Swift to its close ebbs out life's little day.
Earth's joys grow dim; its sorrows pass away,
Change and decay in all around I see,
O, thou who changest not, abide with me.

I remember those two verses still, though not the others, because I sing those verses to my own children. "O, thou who changest not," I sing in the words that have remained with me since

I first learned to speak, "abide with me." I have tried singing all the verses perched on this or that child's bed, but it means hunting the hymnal and leaving on the light; it means taking my eyes from the sweet, sticky face of a child drifting off to sleep and keeping them on the text. It means transforming what is primarily an experience of sound and touch—the night—into a visual experience which belongs rightly to the day.

So I stay with what I know, singing those same two verses again and again, if need be, 'til I feel the child's breathing go long and rhythmic, slowing into sleep beneath my resting hand. "O, thou who changest not," I sing, caressing the body which seems to lengthen and strengthen daily, the delicious folds of baby fat smoothed and hardened by each day of exploration and play. "Abide with me," I sing, in part to God and in part to the child who dreams of living in a space station on the moon or beyond. "Abide with me," I sing to the melody which links me to another child, long ago, lying under the curved glass of an Oldsmobile 88 as it hurtles past the road signs for Hereford and Bovina, Springlake and Sudan.

"Abide with me" I sing in a world which, as any child will tell you, looks different, is different in the dark. Landmarks disappear or are transformed, by hall light or moonlight or oncoming car lights, into threatening shapes and strange figures. The familiar is swallowed up in darkness and we are set adrift in the night. Especially in the first few minutes after we turn off the lights, as our eyes adjust we feel helpless and must cling to other landmarks—tactile and aural—which will re-member us to the place and time, to the people which is our own. Walking in a cave, or through a tunnel, we call out to our companions, relying on the sound of our voices to orient us, one to another. That's what lullabies do: They orient us, one to another. "I am not alone. I cannot see her, but here is her voice, known and near." The words and tunes of lullabies are words and tunes of memory, re‑membering us to our place, even when its familiar outlines are shrouded or changed by darkness and shadows; re‑membering us to our past and to the voices who first sang to us, before words, before conscious memory; re‑membering us to our people whose faces, though hidden, remain.

Pick up a newborn and you will find yourself in motion: rocking, walking, your weight shifting slowly from one foot to another. Then you will begin to sing, and the words, when they

30- come, will be from the sleep songs someone sang to you, words you do not remember learning, words you have always known, words of comfort and promise, words to sing against the darkness as we travel the road toward home.

A man sees, as he dies,
Death's possibilities;
My heart sways with the world.
I am that final thing,
A man learning to sing.

—from "The Dying Man" by Theodore Roethke

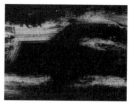

CHAPTER *3*

ARE YOU AWAKE?

God, come to my assistance.
Lord, make haste to help me.

Glory to the Father, and to the Son,
and to the Holy Spirit:
As it was in the beginning, is now,
and will be forever. Amen.

Are you awake?" The hoarse whisper comes less as a question than as a call, a plea. We do not, after all, expect a response from a sleeping person. So the words "Are you awake?" mean: "Please be awake. Don't sleep and leave me alone here in the dark. Please wake up, stay awake, and share my fears, my needs."

So we couch the cry as a question, "Are you awake?" a reflection of our deepest night fear that there will be no answer, that we might, indeed, be left to face the darkness alone. I am roused by the sound of a child's croupy cough in the hours before a winter's dawn. The mother of five, I know the drill: Take the child into the bathroom and turn on all the hot water faucets. Sit in the steam and allow the moist heat to ease the child's barking cough into even breaths. There is nothing more to be done at home, and the physical ratio is right: one parent, one child. Even so, I rouse my husband. "Are you awake?" I know he is not awake and does not wish to be awakened. He is weary, and in need of rest. Still, I shake him and ask again, "Are you awake?" I want him, need him, to be awake, so I tell him, "I'm worried." The coughs are too deep, too loud in a bathroom where no one is jostling for space at the sink, knocking impatiently at the door or bemoaning perceived distortions of teeth, hair and skin before the mirror. It is lonely to be awake with a sick child

when the rest of the world appears to be sleeping. I doubt my judg-
ment in the dark. "Is he getting better? Or should we call the doctor?" I want to know that another hears my questions.

Sometimes my husband will come and sit with us in the
steam clouds. We do not talk, except to soothe our child, but I can
look in his eyes and find a match for the worry in my own.
Sometimes my husband will say, as I say to him in other circumstances, "You know more about this than I do. You'll be fine."

My widowed mother lives alone. By her bed she keeps a late-
twentieth century vigil light: a digital clock radio. She can know the
precise moment of her awakening and keep count of the seconds as
she listens to the night sounds and wonders how to discern the
them: an intruder, or a particularly industrious paper carrier? The

last syncopated beats of an exhausted heart, or the caffeine dance of a heart flushed with forbidden and delicious late-night coffee?

In the wash of the clock light, she can see her speed-dial phone, the gift of children who are not there and who have not been there for decades now. Yet they know that neither age nor solitude erases the need to ask, to know, "Are you awake?" and to understand that there will be company, even in those most solitary hours of her most solitary days.

Of course, my mother does not call any of us in the night. She knows better than to interrupt us for anything less than bleeding or break-ins. Perhaps she lifts the receiver, hesitates, and then replaces it in its plastic cradle. I do not know. We have moved away from the intimacies of night and see one another now only clothed and coiffed, the remembered nocturnal terrors tucked away as neatly as the corners of the bedsheets smoothed of their sleep tangles.

Still, the need persists. We neither outgrow as individuals, nor outlive as communities, the hunger for a companion in the night. We hear our own heart's desire in the words of the psalmist who asks, and then answers, the question:

> *If I look to the mountains,*
> *will they come to my aid?*
> *My help is the Lord,*
> *who made earth and the heavens.*
>
> *May God, ever wakeful,*
> *keep you from stumbling;*

the guardian of Israel
neither rests nor sleeps.

God shields you,
a protector by your side.
The sun shall not harm you by day
nor the moon at night.

God shelters you from evil,
securing your life.
God watches over you near and far,
now and always.

—Psalm 121

The assurance that the guardian of Israel—unlike spouses,
children, roommates or neighbors—never slumbers, never sleeps,
gives us the courage to speak our need as it is: not as a question, not
wheedling or pleading or begging, but as a call to the one who keeps
watch with us in the long hours of the night.

> God, *come to my assistance.*
> Lord, *make haste to help me.*

Only beloved children, children rooted in the assurance of
love, are so bold. There is no hesitation, no apology, no question in
the midnight cry of a child in need. "Mama, I'm sick at my stomach."
"Papa, I need to talk to you. I'm in trouble." In their discomfort,

their dis-ease, they will call "Mama, Papa," and sometimes only that: the name of their comforter, again and again. The smallest ones have no name for their need; the older ones no need to name it: The one who has been called will come.

> *Lord, keep me as the apple of your eye,*
> *Keep me in the shadow of your wings.*

We know who is the apple of one's eye: a beloved child. We know who is sheltered beneath the wings of a mother bird: her young.

The syntax of the church's call to worship reminds us that we are beloved sons and daughters of God. We can be bold. We can put aside our worry that we will disturb slumber: The guardian of

Israel never slumbers, never sleeps. We can cast aside our fears of abandonment in all its forms: The guardian of Israel will watch our going and our coming now and for evermore. We can cease our search for reasons important enough, for words convincing enough to justify a cry in the night. Like cherished children, we can simply speak, speak the name of the comforter, again and again, certain that the One who has been called will come.

We will know loss and longing in the night, but we will not know them alone. We will weep from pain and cry for pity, and our cries will be heard. So in the quiet and unquiet hours of the night we can remember with all the beloved children of God:

With my Christ I have ever been,
With my Christ, I am now,
With my Christ, I will be forever;
In or out of suffering,
*   you only will I confess.*

—Nestor of Magydus

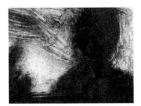

CHAPTER 4

LEARN IN NAKEDNESS

I confess to almighty God,
and to you, my brothers and sisters,
that I have sinned through my own fault
in my thoughts and in my words,
in what I have done,
and in what I have failed to do;
and I ask blessed Mary, ever Virgin,
all the angels and saints,
and you, my brothers and sisters,
to pray for me to the Lord our God.

We got a letter from my aunt, an octogenarian, regarding her burial plans. She wants to "make a good-looking corpse," she writes, as she has always been a good-looking woman. It is true. My aunt, whose youngest child collects Social Security, wears aquamarine-tinted contacts and has her hair colored champagne gold. She is a careful dresser whose silks still slide over her latex-reinforced flesh. At night she wears lounging pajamas with feather-trimmed mules. If our earthly span is like a ship sinking inexorably below the waves, my aunt has chosen passage on the Titanic, where all the doomed will go down in dinner dress while the orchestra plays dance tunes.

For "the viewing" my aunt has chosen a hostess gown. She has the word of her hairdresser that she will not go dark-rooted into that dark night. It is a comfort, my aunt explains, to know that she will be laid out as she lived. Ever a southern lady, my aunt never turned an unadorned face toward a man in her life, and she is not about to make God—of whose masculinity she is certain—the first. She will die, but not without "putting on her face." For my aunt, I think, this is a final act of courtesy, a last gracious offering to the God of all grace.

My childhood friends and I grew up on the tail of that teach-
ing, the one which takes Paul's admonition to women to cover their
heads in church and works downward to include the entire body,
the entire time. By "cover" was meant "artful concealment." Hats
and lace scarves were meant only to cover enough and to cover in
such a way as to enhance what was attractive about one's hair and
face and obscure what was not. Foundation makeup was no veil over
the face but rather a filler for crater-like pores and a paint to hide
eruptions. What remained was meant to be seen, but not in its nakedness, not as it was or is or will be, a human face subject to the sculpt-
ing winds of life and death.

It reminds me of a celebrity who is purported to hand out
to autograph seekers pre-printed business cards affirming that the

bearer has met said personage and found him to be "warm, polite, intelligent and funny," without, of course, any actual exchange—so to speak—of bodily anything. And that is, after all, the point of concealment: to obscure that which we do not wish known ("I am dead, not asleep." "I have pores on my face." "I am a person who is at times cold, rude, block-headed and boring.") while projecting its opposite. Which is what's so hard about intimacy: It requires nakedness.

Sooner or later, lovers stand naked before one another, and not always on purpose with their stomachs sucked in. Husbands and wives pass each other stumbling in or out of the bathroom at 6:00 AM. Men stand watch while their wives, sweating and straining, give birth in nakedness to their naked children. But not to rise from a common bed, rumpled and lined with sleep, not to be present at

the uncovering, the unfolding, the unfurling which is birth, is to
acknowledge a distance which cannot admit nakedness, cannot allow
the intimacy which is our life laid bare. "Love is not love which
alters when it alteration finds," Shakespeare wrote. These are lines I
have cause to ponder as I ponder my southerly drifting flesh. But
what does it mean? That love is only after it has seen one's nakedness and all the alterations of stress and time which we take such
pains to conceal, and remains love?

It is tempting to think of the examination of conscience at
the end of the day as a kind of score sheet—Visitors 5, Home 0—
to be entered into the heavenly ledger, with the end of time as a
final grand and glorious reconciling of the human tally. And, as with
all scores, it is tempting to settle some and contest others. "Yes, I did

smack the baby's bottom, but it was only after . . ." and the argument commences. We uncover, in a strip-tease of the conscience, strategically, and then scramble to gather up and restore our covering. It is too fearsome to admit nakedness.

But nakedness is what we are, in truth, invited into in the examination of conscience. To learn in nakedness is to lie in nakedness, as one lies still under the soft, exploring touch of the beloved, and to reveal oneself—marked, flawed, scarred, misshapen—and begin to understand that the beloved alters not, withdraws never, when it alteration finds.

It is the image Jesus gives us of the prodigal son: ill-clad, ill-fed and having squandered all his father's gifts, embraced in his father's arms, standing close under his father's gaze. The son cannot 55 conceal the toll of the road—its odor, its dusting of grit and streaky sheen of sweat—nor can he produce what he does not have, the lost fortune. With neither the means nor the strength for concealment, the son had to choose: To come at all was to come stripped and naked. Yet the Father does not withdraw or turn away. He sees, and loves.

In word and in deed, our nightly nakedness is like that of this prodigal coming to what we believe is still home: "We lay our earthly garments by, / Upon our beds to rest: / So death will soon disrobe us all / Of all that we possess." Our disrobing is like a return to Paradise, to that ancient but remembered home before clothes were imagined.

I lie in my bed
    As I would lie in my grave,
Thine arm beneath my neck,
    Thou Son of Mary victorious.

—from the Celtic tradition

CHAPTER 5

LIE DOWN IN PEACE

Answer when I call, faithful God.
You cleared away my trouble;
be good to me, listen to my prayer.

How long, proud fools,
will you insult my honor,
loving lies and chasing shadows?
Look! God astounds believers,
the Lord listens when I call.

Tremble, but do not despair.
Attend to your heart,
be calm through the night,
worship with integrity,
trust in the Lord.

Cynics ask, "Who will bless us?
Even God has turned away."
You give my heart more joy

than all their grain and wine.
I sleep secure at night,
you keep me in your care.

—Psalm 4

Some years ago a friend of our daughter's lay very ill in the hospital. A treatment had gone horribly awry, spiraling out of the control of all—doctors, nurses, researchers, therapists—who stood with the child's parents in a vigil that blurred the boundaries of nights and days. No one other than medical personnel and the parents were allowed in the room where they watched, waiting for a sign that would mark the return to life or the descent into death.

We waited at home. This was Anna Kate's best friend, with whom she had just completed first grade, with whom she had grand future plans for careers either in the movies or as nurses, and more immediate plans for a profitable lemonade stand on the corner, just above the storm sewer, right by Libby's house. We wrote letters and drew pictures and baked cookies during the day, all to be kept until Libby could enjoy them. The day had its own work, and its own purposes.

It was at night that the questions came, questions about hospitals and diseases and doctors. We talked about IV's and antibiotics and respiratory therapy, a world mercifully alien to Anna Kate but cruelly familiar to her friend. Finally, the question around which we had been dancing, graceful as waltzers on a stage: "Is Libby going to die?"

Anna Kate asked me as I tucked her in tight, as if by securing the blanket ends I could secure her against all harm. My task completed, I had nothing to do but sit on that taut bed and look into Anna Kate's clear brown eyes.

"Is Libby going to die?" she asked again. I knelt and I took her hand, desperate for a comforting lie and unable to find one in those eyes.

"I don't know, Anna Kate," I said. "I hope not. I pray not, but I don't know."

She began to cry then, her own hopes shattered. She knew me to be somewhat unsympathetic and matter-of-fact about aches and bruises, scratches and contusions. "You don't need a Band-Aid.

Leave it open to the air" was one familiar prescription, as was "Fever is the body's way of handling infection. Just let it be." All of these, unless I had been foolish enough to buy Band-Aids with designs on them, usually suited Anna Kate well enough. Cuts did heal, and sore throats did feel better with nothing more than hot tea and honey. So this admission frightened her, and sent tears spilling over her lashes and onto her cheeks.

"What can we do?" she asked. Mothers do things, in Anna Kate's world. They do things—mop up spills, kiss scrapes, divide the pie into even eighths—and life is better.

"We can pray for Libby," I answered. "We can pray that God's will for Libby be healing and wholeness."

I could not promise that was, or would be, God's will. For
Anna Kate, it was rather like finding out that the one who has pre-
sented herself as Walt Disney's sole heir and the holder of unlimited
movie passes is in fact the cinema concession clerk, whose only pull
is $6.00 plunked down at the ticket window, same as everybody else.

Then I remembered the unlikely garden Libby and her sister
had planted in a narrow patch of dirt by the garage. There were
young tomato plants in a row and marigolds seeded around them to
discourage the tomato bugs. The tomatoes, planted with such hope
and such visions of late-summer salads adorned with the freshly-
picked fruit, were no longer anyone's priority.

"And we can stake the tomato plants," I said, "and water
them." That, at least, was something to be done—a work to be

undertaken when works everywhere had failed, a work which held the promise of growth and ripening, a fruit-bearing work in a barren time. So Anna Kate trembled that night, but she did not despair. She slept.

The psalmist admonishes us to tremble on our beds. Tremble, as we remember those who sleep on heating grates or in discarded refrigerator cartons; tremble, as we remember those whose hunger drives away sleep, whose pain denies rest. Tremble, as we consider those for whom the night has become a hunting ground where both the stalker and the stalked are prey. God, the good father, the loving mother, does not lie to the children who ask for truth. "Is there danger? Danger unto death?" The answer is yes, and the one who is listening, who hears the answer, trembles, rightly.

"Tremble," the psalmist sings, "but do not despair. Attend to your heart." To tremble is to acknowledge the death which is all about us in the night; to despair is to acknowledge death's primacy, its sovereignty over the night. But this night song reminds us that God is faithful, listening when we call, answering when we call, and calling us to the works of light and life in the midst of darkness and death. We are not to despair; there is work to be done, fruit-bearing work in the narrow patch of dirt we have been given to till and to tend. We are to attend to the new growth, the tender shoots started by God in that most unlikely garden, the human heart.

The psalmist promises that cynics will scoff, unimpressed by the spotty evidence of cultivation in a land overrun with prickly weeds and thorns. It is the question I asked even as I comforted my daughter.

"Who cares about that strip of soil when Libby may be dying?"

Well, Libby and her sister did. And so, it seems to me now, did God, does God, who reminds us that life and death do not belong to us and are not in our control, but that the work of life is ours.

"What can we do?" my Anna Kate asked.

And the psalmist answers, "We can attend to our hearts, staking and rooting deep within them the love of God and of God's creatures. We can tend the patch of earth we have been given, working there while it is yet day." And then we can rest, "secure at night," because God keeps it and us in such care.

Fountain of light, source of light,
Hear our prayer.
Drive away from us the shadow of sin.
Seek us, kindly light.

You, who created us in holiness,
Who condemned our sin,
Who redeemed us from our sin,
Sustain us by your power.

The labor of the day is over,
And now we rest safely at home.
Make this home your home,
And protect us with your grace.

The sun has fallen below the earth,
And now the darkness is here.
Let your uncreated light shine
Upon our dark and weary souls.

Pour your gentle light into our dull minds,
Filling our heads with holy thoughts.
Pour your glorious light into our cold breasts,
Kindling holy love within our hearts.

From horror, lust and fear,
Guard us while we sleep.
And if we cannot sleep,
Let our eyes behold your heavenly host.

—Alcuin of York

CHAPTER 6

TO SURROUND THIS NIGHT

All you sheltered by the Most High,
who live in Almighty God's shadow,
say to the Lord, "My refuge, my fortress,
my God in whom I trust!"

God will free you from hunters' snares,
will save you from deadly plague,
will cover you like a nesting bird.
God's wings will shelter you.

No nighttime terror shall you fear,
no arrows shot by day,
no plague that prowls the dark,
no wasting scourge at noon.

A thousand may fall at your side,
ten thousand at your right hand.
But you shall live unharmed:
God is sturdy armor.

You have only to open your eyes
to see how the wicked are repaid.
You have the Lord as refuge,
have made the Most High your stronghold.

No evil shall ever touch you,
no harm come near your home.
God instructs angels
to guard you wherever you go.

With their hands they support you,
so your foot will not strike a stone.
You will tread on lion and viper,
trample tawny lion and dragon.

I deliver all who cling to me,
raise the ones who know my name,
answer those who call me,
stand with those in trouble.
These I rescue and honor,
satisfy with long life,
and show my power to save.

—Psalm 91

There comes a time when toddlers fancy themselves too big for the baby seat in the grocery cart: They would much rather walk alongside the cart, their fingers reaching for boxes of breakfast cereal and jars of jam. The urgent supermarket call, "We need a wet clean-up in aisle seven," is familiar to every parent and small child who have ever stood in a puddle of broken glass and floating food, the debris of childhood curiosity.

I remember our Mary Margaret, whose joy it was to walk by my side through the store until she spied someone—an adult—too large, too loud or too close. Threatened, Mary Margaret would scoot under my skirt and hide. She would maneuver herself between my legs, her head wedged against the sides of my knees and her hands clasped around my calves. I've worn long, full denim skirts for years, unknowingly creating a portable tent for the small children in my care. It must have been dim under those skirts, and warm, a shadowy place where Mary Margaret could stand—unobserved, so she thought—and hear the conversation around her. She could peek out from under the hem once in a while and decide whether to emerge or retreat while I engaged the scary grown-up in curious grown-up talk. My skirts gave her a safe place to hide during those first years of independent exploration and discovery, a retreat when the discoveries proved too much to bear.

I remember the day Mary Margaret spied her pediatrician in the grocery store. She liked him well enough, in the same way she liked the tigers in the zoo: in context. He belonged in his office where, she believed, he was kept. Our little Betsy had explained it all to her smaller sister: Dr. Jones was married to Shirley, the office nurse, the two of them living in that place of throat swabs and thermometers. To see him roaming the produce section shocked Mary Margaret as thoroughly as if she had seen a bear browsing through the bakery. The sight of Dr. Jones might have been more shocking, for no bear had ever stuck her with a needle. She saw Dr. Jones and stopped, then scurried under my skirts, draping herself in a den of

soft cotton, its fibers permeated with the smell of safety and the
scent of her mother. And there she stayed, resting in the shadows,
while the threat of a doctor loose in the world passed and she felt
ready to venture forth once more.

We come to the end of the day in need of shelter and of rest.
The psalmist reminds us that there is such a place for the beloved
children of the Most High and invites us to enter under the skirts of
God. Because God, the psalmist writes, is like a nesting bird, a
mothering bird who covers her young from those who would hunt
them down and kill them, ensnare them and consume them. She
spreads her wings like a swirling skirt and settles them over her children. They wait in the dimness, comforted by the smell of safety, the

scent of their mother and the feel of her flesh. The children cling to her, and she to them. And they are not afraid.

Mary Margaret, like her older siblings, soon abandoned my shadow, finding it no longer comforting but rather confining and constricting. She is now in that realm of adolescence where the charm of life is to walk uncovered, unprotected, in the full glare of life's light. She dismisses my worries as excessive and encourages me to risk more, dare more. I haven't the words to make her understand that I have lived this life with the recklessness of a rock climber without a rope harness. I hang above the abyss of my daring, my daring to birth these children and love them so. How less protected could I be? Like the southern kudzu vine, which sinks its roots into the mortar of buildings, these children have sunk their roots into my heart, entwining themselves with a force and covering that frail organ with a thickness that makes my heart hurt for love of them, for longing to keep them unwounded and well. It is a risky thing to see them off each morning, and a relief and a wonder to welcome them back each night. I know the guilty pleasure of hearing a siren when my children are all in bed downstairs, the unwholesome satisfaction that accompanies the hateful mantra, "Someone else's child. Some other father's son. Some other mother's daughter." Too fierce this love, too cruel in its insistence that we work without nets.

Psalm 91 reads like a catalog of motherfears: the deadly plague, the daytime shot, the night prowlers, the wasting scourge. There are stones in the road and wild beasts; thousands, tens of thousands fall every day. This is not a tall man in the cereal aisle of the grocery store; this is the hunter with his snare. And my skirts have been revealed for what they are: rags, bits of fabric sewn together with thin strands of cotton, draped upon an unimposing frame—not sturdy armor, not armor at all.

Where are we to go? Where are we to point our children— toward the day when their exuberance fades, or is shattered, and they long to rest in faithful shade? We point them, with the psalmist, to the wings of God, to the mother whose strength and wisdom does not fail and who speaks the desire of every mother's heart: that her children shall live unharmed. We offer them the sturdy armor of:

The Sacred Three

To save

To shield

To surround

The hearth

The house

The household

This eve

This night

And every night

Each single night. Amen.

—traditional Gaelic prayer

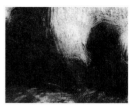

CHAPTER 7

TO THY FAITHFUL ONES, SEVENFOLD HALLOWING

Bless the Lord,
all who serve in God's house,
who stand watch
throughout the night.

Lift up your hands
in the holy place
and bless the Lord.

And may God,
the maker of earth and sky
bless you from Zion.

—Psalm 134

I never asked her how she knew it was time. I lived far away then, and heard on the day I was called back to Amarillo simply that Sharon had brought my brother, Mike, home to die.

She took him home to the bed where Jason had been conceived, where they had read the Sunday morning comics aloud to their little boys, where Mike had lain after chemotherapy, rising only to vomit before returning to the drugged, depleted state which was not sleep, but was yet welcome. She took him home to the bed I had crawled into on the night Jason was born, one February night when it was cold, too cold to wake baby Jeff and bring him to me. I drove over and slipped drowsily into the hollow of sheets and blankets, still warm from their bodies, and slept again until Mike came whispering, "It's a boy. We've got a little boy. Jeff's got a brother." Sharon brought Mike to that bed—his bed, their bed—to die.

Mike did not die at once. He was young, and his body struggled for its rightful span of years. During the long nights of his dying, Sharon rested on the floor beside him, laying on what my family has always called—its origins lost in our Southern past—a "Baptist pallet." Sharon lay beside him like the anxious mother of a newborn child: listening for each breath, willing the life air in and out, in and out. She dozed and roused, awake more often than not, all through those last nights, keeping watch in her home, over her home, while that which she loved and longed to keep slipped away.

It is hard for me to imagine Mike's thoughts as he felt his body dying. What I can imagine is how weary Sharon must have been: up all night, up still in the morning for two young sons who needed breakfast and clean underwear and the permission slips for their field trips signed. Parent-teacher conferences were not canceled while my brother died; math homework in the fifth grade was not suspended. Sharon did what the psalmist sings: She stood night after night, and there was no rest—not then, and not for a long time to come.

I think of her when I hear this psalm, and it makes me tired. Who can lift up hands in the night, when we long to drop our hands, unclench our fists and drift into the unguarded and unbidden life of sleep? Who can stand night after night when we are beckoned by the sweet, slow slide between cool sheets? It is not hymns we desire but the low groan of pleasure that escapes our lips as we settle into the mattress and bunch the pillow into shape. Our dreaming thoughts take us to the halls of elementary school where we appear naked in spelling bees; clad only in underwear for the Pledge of Allegiance. Our limbs move restlessly in a dark unconscious dance. Life does not stop at night, but we sleepers can relinquish responsibility for our lives. And it is with relish that, in our last waking thoughts, we are aware of the letting go.

It is that delight Anna Kate and I consider as she goes to bed, especially on snowy nights. Her bedroom, a converted sleeping porch on the second floor of our house, features a half-wall of windows. In bed, she can watch the flakes drift on our neighbor's roof. I tuck her in, and we talk about the pleasures of a warm bed on a cold night. That talk leads us to consider those who must be out in the weather, out in the darkness—because they have no homes or because their work demands it—and those who will be awake in the night: the lonely, the lost, the grieving, the fearful, the sick, the dying and those who keep watch with them. We ask the Lord, maker of heaven and earth, as the psalmist does, to bless them, and us. Those who lie down in peace and those who stand night after night—may we be blessed, may we be blessed from Zion.

What is soiled cleanse
What is dry refresh
What is wounded heal.

What is rigid bend
What is frozen warm
Guide what goes astray.

Give thy faithful ones
Who in thee confide
Sevenfold hallowing.

Give goodness its reward
Give journey safe through death
Give joy that has no end.

Lava quod est sordidum,
Riga quod est aridum,
Sana quod est saucium.

Flecte quod est rigidum,
Fove quod est frigidum,
Rege quod est devium.

Da tuis fidelibus,
In te confidentibus,
Sacrum septenarium.

Da virtutis meritum,
Da salutis exitum,
Da perenne gaudium.

—a thirteenth century hymn, translated by George Appleton

CHAPTER 8

WAIT IN WONDER

I am serene because I know thou lovest me.

Because thou lovest me,

nought can move me from my peace.

Because thou lovest me,

I am one to whom all good has come.

    — from the Celtic tradition

It happened three years ago, on the first Sunday of Advent. Our parish staff had erected a "giving tree" near the entrance to the church, as is the custom. Recycled cards from Christmases past hung from the branches. On each card was written a request: "Girl, age 4, wants something pretty" or "Boy, age 13, needs snow boots," and then the size of the recipient.

Betsy chose a card from a thirteen-year-old girl who wanted a pair of then newly fashionable stirrup pants. No matter that the pants might be out of style in a season: Betsy wanted—wants— no part of drab righteousness. It would be fun and fashionable or it would not be worthy of the name "gift." Her younger sisters were, as they always are, watching.

Mary Margaret chose a card from a twelve-year-old girl who needed a sweater to wear to school. "I'll know what to pick," Mary Margaret said, "I know what kind of sweater she'll like."

We chose, by acclamation, a card for Andrew from a two-year-old boy who wanted "a toy that makes noise." Andrew, little Andrew, who was once carried out of the Christmas Eve Mass merrily shouting "Jingle Balls" all the way down the center aisle, was then both a creator and a connoisseur of noise.

Abram was struck by a card that read: "Girl, age 16—maternity top, size 9." Underneath the typed information was hand-written: "Mom kicked her out—she's staying with her grandmother." He chose that one.

Anna Kate found her card after a careful search through the branches. It read: "Girl, age 5, ice cream maker."

I was well-versed in ice cream makers that year, because Anna Kate wanted one for Christmas. And because Anna Kate, who is magic, wanted an ice cream maker, Andrew wanted one, too. I knew that, even at a discount store, such a toy would cost about thirty dollars. I was very aware of the large investment—in money, soap and patience—one of those gadgets would require.

The children of the poor must learn early to make sober and modest requests. Advent after Advent, the cards on our parish tree list requests for mittens or ski caps or footed pajamas, the sort of sensible and worthwhile gifts people like me are willing to give. For I am in favor of charity, though never charity at the expense of my own wants and needs or those of my immediate biological family. And while thirty dollars is not too much to spend on my own sweet child, it seems a bit much for some stranger's son or daughter.

So I tried to steer Anna Kate to the "socks" or "sleepers" cards, disguising my penury with the concerned tone of one who wants only the best for a child whose toes might otherwise be cold in the mountain air. Besides, I knew socks were fifty percent off at Target.

But Anna Kate had glimpsed a kindred spirit, another little
girl who waited as Anna waited—for something wonderful. She saw
someone else who imagined herself playing restaurant with real
frosties and ice cream cones. Anna Kate thought she knew this girl,
a child who wanted what she herself wanted, a child who dared to
dream of a gift lacking all utility, unless one counts as useful, joy.

Anna Kate held tight to her card, which I have kept. I've
kept it as a reminder to me of the extravagance of God's love and
the poverty of my own. I kept it as a reminder of the difference
between the English word "waiting" and "esperando," a Spanish
word I learned that season which means both "waiting" and "hoping."

"Another day, another dollar," my husband will sometimes
sigh as he settles himself for sleep. And so it often seems: the day

is given over to getting and keeping, the night to preparing for another day. Perhaps we sleep; perhaps we lie awake in the darkness plotting the work of the day undawned or mourning the work undone in the day just past. Children of another sort of poverty, we are sober and sensible and circumscribed in our longings: "If I can make it to the post office before nine . . . If I could only get seven hours of sleep before the alarm rings at six."

We are all socks and mittens, all utility and common sense. What place does Simeon's Song have in our nightly routine? We are waiting for a buzzer (with perhaps a five-minute snooze alarm as our only concession to wild abandon) and Simeon is waiting—for what? Simeon is waiting like a child who still dares to ask for "something pretty." Simeon is waiting for something wonderful.

All we know of Simeon from the writer of Luke's Gospel is that "he was just and pious" and that he was waiting for something: "the consolation of Israel . . . the Announced of the Lord." Simeon would not die, he had been told, until he beheld God's "saving deed," until he held Jesus in his arms and blessed God with these words:

Lord let your servant
now die in peace,
for you kept your promise.

With my own eyes
I see the salvation
you prepared for all peoples:

light revealing life to the Gentiles
and glory to your people Israel.

Simeon's Song is extravagant, lush, lusty even—all that display and glory, all that revelation and light. What does it have to do with the beds of working Americans, who only lie down to get up and do it all over again? ("Could you keep it down out there?" I imagine yelling at the giddy old man, "Some of us have to work in the morning!") Deliverance from the terrors of the night, we understand. Wanting one's mother, or crying out for forgiveness, for peace—these are needs of the night we understand.

But to fall asleep like an adored child on Christmas Eve, to fall asleep certain that the word of a loving parent will be fulfilled,

to fall asleep certain that our eyes will close only to open before
glory—is more than our impoverished hearts can hold. For we've
shrunk our hearts in the bracing cold water wash of what we like to
call reality. And reality is the final bullet-riddled report on the late
local news, a lullaby of warning to lock up and watch out, a valedic-
tory which turns the night into a wait without hope, without joy.
Batten down the hatches and shrink, small and ever smaller, to be a
less inviting target. Never dare to ask for more than one can reasonably expect: to awake and to work.

Yet the ancient night tradition of us Christians is to go to
sleep with Simeon's bold words on our lips. We pass from wakefulness
to sleep with the daring declaration of who we are: men and women

whose longings for abundance—not subsistence, but abundance—will be fulfilled in our hearing and in our sight, upon our hungry lips and along our eager flesh.

There is always a watch, a waiting, in the night. We wait for the sun's return, for the ascent into consciousness. Simeon's song calls us to *esperando,* to wait with hope—for something wonderful, for the sure and certain coming of our Beloved.

The eternal kingdom is within sight,
  a kingdom that shall suffer no loss.
Lord Jesus Christ, we are Christians,
  we are your servants;
You alone are our hope,
  the hope of all Christians.
God almighty, God most high:
  we give you praise,
  we give praise to your name.

—Thelica of Abitine

CHAPTER 9

FOLD HOME THY CHILD

We place ourselves in your keeping,
    holy Mother of God.
Refuse not the prayer of your children
        in their distress,
but deliver us from all danger,
ever virgin, glorious and blessed.

—the "Sub tuum"

Last winter, television cameras were turned on a Midwestern house where 19 children lived. The adults in the house had neither the time nor the energy, nor, it would seem, the will to tend the children they had borne. The news report, though distressing, was not startling. Stories of the stabbing, starving, scalding and bludgeoning of children are common fare on television news. What startled me was the question of one small girl to the officer who was leading her out of the house: "Will you be my mommy?"

This child was inarticulate in the way of the very young, but this is what she clearly knew: I need a mother. The child had some image, some vision of a mother—this, she stubbornly sought. Perhaps the officer fed her or comforted her or changed her soiled clothes for clean, or wiped her nose or knelt close to explain the confusing sights and sounds of a police raid. Perhaps she did what mothers are supposed to do, and the little girl responded. Perhaps she took her hand for safe-keeping, or caressed her head, and the little girl felt that here was the one she had been seeking.

It reminded me of my father, who, as he lay dying, called for his mother. Theirs had been a turbulent relationship, kept off balance by my father's wasteful ways and his expectation that my grandmother should, could and would rescue him from his excesses.

He was never the son for whom she had hoped, nor was she the mother he had desired, but in that final closing of his eyes, he called for her alone. It is what I, the flawed mother of five, have learned from countless sleep-overs that have ended prematurely in tears and scary dreams of monsters and upset stomachs: In the night, distressed children want their mothers.

My children, whom I have wounded, want me. Their wounds are hidden, of no interest to a television crew or to Social Services, but their wounds are real. I imagine them as slight thicknesses lining the once-smooth surfaces of their hearts, much as the human face grows lined and thickened from the assaults of wind and sun. But the assaults upon my children have come not from the unthinking elements but from the one whose very name means trust and succor— from their mother, from me. I have entertained guests with stories that my children never meant to leave the bedside confessional; I have spilled secrets which seep into the weaving of our lives like spilled blood, never to be washed out, a stain, a scar. I have taught them to be wary of "Mama's bad moods," her hurt feelings, her injured airs. I have taken the scattered buckshot of adolescent sarcasm and returned it as armor-piercing bullets, my tongue so much longer trained in the withering retort than their own. My anger has blazed up, and I have seen fear in their eyes, heard, "Mama, please don't be mad; I'm really sorry" from lips never meant to beg my affection, lips never meant to ask, "Will you still be my mother, the mother I need," the mother I can so seldom be, so seldom am.

We all want our mothers, as they are or were, might have been or ought to have been. Those of us whose mothers are dead want them back, healed and whole. Those of us abandoned by our mothers want them back, healed and whole, loving and beloved. Those of us whose mothers were hurtful or careless want them still, need them still, though we long for the mother's help and caring so long denied. And those of us whose mothers were wise and kind want them still.

Especially in the falling dark, when the darkness seems impenetrable, we want our mothers. There is a link between the mothering presence, the mothering presence as we wish her to be and the needs of the night.

Sleep, my child, and peace attend thee,
All through the night . . .
I my loving vigil keeping,
All through the night.

    The words of this old Welsh lullaby speak to the needs of the night. The singer urges sleep and promises peace, can promise peace, because the slumberer will not be abandoned to the darkness. The singer will keep watch, a loving vigil, through the night hours, indeed "all through the night." The "I" who sings, who waits by the bedside, is never identified, but the high soprano melody to which the words are set and the words themselves tell us that this is a mother, the mother each of us seeks, who croons her quiet pledge. It is the mother who invites us to place ourselves in her keeping and assures us that there we will be safe, delivered from all danger.

I remember nights spent on the floor beside the bed of a sick and feverish child, a child passing in and out of uncomfortable sleep. I could not stop the coughing or the vomiting and I have been reluctant to stop the necessary work of the infection-destroying fever. I have been helpless before the pain. But when the child awoke and cried out, I could say, "Ssh, it's all right, Mama's here. I'm right here," sure in the understanding that this was what both of us needed to hear, and know.

It is this need of the night we acknowledge and honor in the hymn to Mary.

Be thou then, O thou dear
Mother, my atmosphere;
My happier world, wherein
To wend and meet no sin;
Above me, round me lie
Fronting my froward eye
With sweet and scarless sky;
Stir in my ears, speak there
Of God's love, O live air,
Of patience, penance, prayer:
Worldmothering air, air wild,
Wound with thee, in thee isled,
Fold home, fast fold thy child.

—Gerard Manley Hopkins

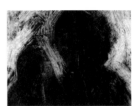

CHAPTER 10

THE FINAL BLESSING

The Lord grant us a quiet night and a perfect end.

—*Compline*

I began, nearly twenty years ago now, to mark my children with the sign of the cross. Lying in bed, just before sleep, they can feel my thumb as it traces the strokes—now down, now across—of their true shape and rightful belonging. I sign them as I did on the day of their baptism, a first and final blessing. I sign them as I did the toddler Andrew, who, unable to catch the rhythm of the signing before the proclamation of the Gospel at Mass, would whisper, "Do me,

Mama, do me." But as the children pass into adolescence, it is a gesture that feels right to them only in the dark. In the light, this sign becomes a brand of another sort.

It is my experience that teenagers leaving for rafting trips or orchestra tours do not wish to be signed on the forehead with the cross. They do not wish it as they do not wish to have "geek" printed across their foreheads in red permanent marker. There is a danger of smeared make-up, of oily thumbs on freshly de-oiled skin, of hooking a careful curl and messing up the mousse. There is a danger of being associated with someone who looks like the sort of plump, middle-aged woman who opens her refrigerator to find the Virgin Mary staring back at her out of the strawberry Jell—O. "It looks," my daughter Betsy told me, "so religious."

I have persevered, and so have my teenage children. I have -123
aimed and they have ducked, flinched, grimaced, bobbed and weaved.
They have held up their hands to ward me off much like characters
in B-movies attempt to ward off the werewolf. I have signed foreheads wrinkled in disgust and impatience. I have signed shoulders
and forearms and tops of heads and cheeks and ears and necks, any-
where my thumb could land on their agile, fleeing forms. I have
signed Betsy under the cover of her ski jacket, making us appear, no
doubt, like a matronly dealer and her sweet-faced junkie complet-
ing a deal. I have walked Abram to the far reaches of an unfinished
airport concourse so that I might sign him in secrecy. I have had
Mary Margaret close her fingers gently around my upraised wrist and

assure me, as one assures those who need to find a hobby, get a job, get a life, put down the knife, "Mom, it's all right."

When Abram left for college, the first of our five to leave, he came to me and solemnly, silently, inclined his head. We stood there awkwardly for a moment, him waiting for me, me wondering what to do. I thought perhaps he wanted me to check for dandruff or some other scalp or skin condition. Then I realized what he was waiting for, what he was asking for: his blessing.

And I was at last able to reach forward slowly and make that most graceful of Christian gestures with deliberation and care. "Abram," I said, "go with God. In the name of the Father, and of the Son, and of the Holy Spirit." It had been a long time coming, that bending of his stiff, adolescent neck, that inclining of his head toward my hand upraised in blessing.

So slowly does the heart turn that we cannot detect the movement. And so little do we trust that we despair of what we cannot see. It is that way with me. "Eighteen years," I lay in bed that night and thought, "eighteen years is almost half of my life, and he just now comes to ask for his blessing."

It is hard for me now to remember my expectations as a new mother. Any memory of those expectations is overlaid with what I have experienced and learned. But I don't think I ever reckoned with the creep of human formation. Never did I anticipate that so much of my adult life would be spent crouched before a toilet chirping, "Good boy! Have you got any more?" or "That's such a big girl!"

Never did I anticipate that I would spend years repeating, "We don't hit" to children who clearly did, and with gusto. (I once enlarged on my "no hitting" homily with what I felt to be an age-appropriate theological reflection on the life of Christ, who was known to heal and feed and teach and bless, but never, ever to hit. "And," I added piously, "Jesus wants us to be just like him." To which my three-year-old Andrew responded reasonably, "Well, Jesus didn't *like* to hit; but I *do*.") I have asked, "What do you say?" so often that I find the words bouncing around in my head when a store clerk or mechanic I have thanked doesn't tell me I am welcome. And I do find myself cautioning children I encounter for the first time in parking lots to "watch out for cars, sweetie; don't dart out into the lot" even when their own watchful parents are standing by. I suppose it explains

why my own mother, who never saw a car seat until her first grand-
child was strapped into one, still flings out her right arm to stop me,
her baby from the fifties, from flying into the dashboard when we
come to a quick stop—except that I, seat-belted, usually drive now
when we are together. She sits on my right these days and so must
switch arms, but the gesture endures.

I don't recall what I expected, but I know what I have
learned. And I have learned it slowly and through constant repetition, as people do. This is what I have learned: that our necks are
stiff and unbending, and that it takes time and grace before we learn
to incline them to one another and to God.

We ask at night for a perfect end, but that does not preclude
a journey to our perfect end filled with imperfections. Do not be

discouraged. Learning to pray at night, learning to put aside, as the writer of Hebrews says, "every weight and all that hinders us"—will be learned as is all of life, slowly and through constant repetition. A night follows every day, through all the days of our lives. And each one is given to us to learn, to learn the feel of our true shape, to learn the sound of our rightful belongings. A whole lifetime full of nights, given to us by God, who knows how slowly the human heart turns, how reluctantly the closed fist opens, with what difficulty the rigid neck bends. A whole lifetime full of nights, given to us by the Beloved who watches over them all, who watches over us all in never-ending story.

Servant of God, remember
The stream thy soul bedewing,
The grace that came upon thee
Anointing and renewing.

When kindly slumber calls thee
Upon thy bed reclining,
Trace thou the cross of Jesus,
Thy heart and forehead signing.

The cross dissolves the darkness,
And drives away temptation;
It calms the wavering spirit
By quiet consecration.

Then while the weary body
Its rest in sleep is nearing,
The heart will muse in silence
On Christ and Christ's appearing.

To God, eternal Father,
To Christ, our King, be glory,
And to the Holy Spirit,
In never-ending story.

—Prudentius, Compline hymn

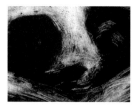

THE NIGHT PRAYER OF THE CHURCH

The texts of many prayers are given throughout this book. Some are gathered here in a traditional order of night prayer. In addition to texts, which are usually known by heart and may be sung, chanted or recited, the night prayer needs silence, gestures like the sign of the cross or a bow, and sometimes an appropriate posture such as kneeling or standing.

132- *Make the sign of the cross and say:*

God, come to my assistance.
Lord, make haste to help me.

Or:

Protect us, Lord, as we stay awake;
watch over us as we sleep,
that, awake, we may keep watch with Christ,
and, asleep, rest in Christ's peace.

After some quiet, a prayer for God's mercy:

I confess to almighty God,
and to you, my brothers and sisters,

that I have sinned through my own fault
in my thoughts and in my words,
in what I have done,
and in what I have failed to do;
and I ask blessed Mary, ever virgin,
all the angels and saints,
and you, my brothers and sisters,
to pray for me to the Lord our God.

Or:

May almighty God have mercy on us,
forgive us our sins,
and bring us to everlasting life.

A psalm or a canticle is prayed:

Psalm 4

Answer when I call, faithful God.
You cleared away my trouble;
be good to me, listen to my prayer.

How long, proud fools,
will you insult my honor,
loving lies and chasing shadows?
Look! God astounds believers,
the Lord listens when I call.

Tremble, but do not despair.
Attend to your heart,
be calm through the night,
worship with integrity,
trust in the Lord.

Cynics ask, "Who will bless us?
Even God has turned away."
You give my heart more joy
than all their grain and wine.
I sleep secure at night,
you keep me in your care.

Psalm 91

All you sheltered by the Most High,
who live in Almighty God's shadow,
say to the Lord, "My refuge, my fortress,
my God in whom I trust!"

God will free you from hunters' snares,
will save you from deadly plague,
will cover you like a nesting bird.
God's wings will shelter you.

No nighttime terror shall you fear,
no arrows shot by day,

no plague that prowls the dark,
no wasting scourge at noon.

A thousand may fall at your side,
ten thousand at your right hand.
But you shall live unharmed:
God is sturdy armor.

You have only to open your eyes
to see how the wicked are repaid.
You have the Lord as refuge,
have made the Most High your stronghold.

138-   No evil shall ever touch you,
         no harm come near your home.
         God instructs angels
         to guard you wherever you go.

         With their hands they support you,
         so your foot will not strike a stone.
         You will tread on lion and viper,
         trample tawny lion and dragon.

         "I deliver all who cling to me,
         raise the ones who know my name,
         answer those who call me,
         stand with those in trouble.

These I rescue and honor,
satisfy with long life,
and show my power to save."

Psalm 131

Lord, I am not proud,
holding my head too high,
reaching beyond my grasp.

No, I am calm and tranquil
like a weaned child
resting in its mother's arms:
my whole being at rest.

Let Israel rest in the Lord,
now and for ever.

Psalm 134

Bless the Lord,
all who serve in God's house,
who stand watch
throughout the night.

Lift up your hands
in the holy place
and bless the Lord.

And may God,
the maker of earth and sky,
bless you from Zion.

Canticle of Simeon

Lord, let your servant
now die in peace,
for you kept your promise.

With my own eyes
I see the salvation
you prepared for all peoples:

a light of revelation for the Gentiles
and glory to your people Israel.

A song may be sung.

Abide with me! fast falls the eventide;
The darkness deepens, Lord with me abide;
When other helpers fail; and comfort flee,
Help of the helpless, oh, abide with me!

Swift to its close ebbs out life's little day;
Earth's joys grow dim; its glories pass away;
Change and decay in all around I see;
O God, the changeless one, abide with me!

I fear no foe, with you at hand to bless;
Ills have no weight, and tears no bitterness:
Where is death's sting? Where, grace, your victory?
I triumph still, if you abide with me!

Day is done, but Love unfailing
Dwells ever here;
Shadows fall, but hope, prevailing,
Calms ev'ry fear.
Loving Father, none forsaking,
Take our hearts, of Love's own making
Watch our sleeping, guard our waking,
Be always near!

144- Dark descends, but Light unending
Shines through our night;
You are with us, ever lending
New strength to sight;
One in love, your truth confessing,
One in hope of heaven's blessing,
May we see, in love's possessing'
Love's endless light!

Eyes will close, but you, unsleeping,
Watch by our side;
Death may come: in Love's safe keeping
Still we abide.

God of love, all evil quelling,
Sin forgiving, fear dispelling,
Stay with us, our hearts indwelling,
This eventide!

O Christ, you are the light and day
Which drives away the night,
The ever shining Sun of God
And pledge of future light.

As now the evening shadows fall
O grant us, Lord, we pray,
A quiet night to rest in you
Until the break of day.

146- Regard, O Lord, our helplessness
And come to our defense;
May we be governed by your love,
In true obedience.

Remember us, poor mortals all,
We humbly ask, O Lord
And may your presence in our souls
Be now our great reward.

Lord Jesus Christ, abide with us,
Now that the sun has run its course;
Let hope not be obscured by night
But may faith's darkness be as light.

Lord Jesus Christ, grant us the your peace,
And when the trials of earth shall cease;
Grant us the morning light of grace,
The radiant splendor of your face.

Immortal, holy three-fold light,
Yours be the kingdom, pow'r and might;
All glory be eternally
To you, life-giving Trinity.

All praise to you, O God, this night,
For all the blessings of the light;
Keep us, we pray, O King of kings,
Beneath your own almighty wings.

148- Forgive us, Lord, through Christ your Son
Whatever wrong this day we've done;
Your peace give to the world, O Lord,
That all might live in one accord.

Teach me to live that I may dread
The grave as little as my bed;
Teach me to die that so I may
Rise glorious of that final day.

Enlighten us, O blessed Light.
And give us rest throughout this night.
O strengthen us, that for your sake,
We all may serve you when we wake.

Night prayer concludes with this prayer and with
the invocation to Mary:

Visit this house,
we beg you, Lord,
and banish from it
the deadly power of the evil one.
May your holy angels dwell here
to keep us in peace,
and may your blessing be always upon us.

Hail, holy Queen, Mother of mercy,
hail, our life, our sweetness, and our hope!
To you we cry, the children of Eve;

150- to you we send up our sighs,
mourning and weeping in this land of exile.
Turn, then, most gracious advocate,
your eyes of mercy toward us;
lead us home at last
and show us the blessed fruit of your womb, Jesus:
O clement, O loving, O sweet Virgin Mary.

Make the sign of the cross and say:

May the almighty and merciful Lord,
the Father and the Son and the Holy Spirit,
bless and keep us.

Or:

Keep us, O Lord, as the apple of your eye.
Shelter us in the shadow of your wings.

Or:

Into your hands, Lord, I commend my spirit.

ACKNOWLEDGMENTS

The English translation of the psalms and the Canticle of Simeon are from *The Liturgical Psalter*. Copyright © 1994 by the International Committee on English in the Liturgy, Inc. (ICEL). Used with permission. All rights reserved.

"I Am Lying Down Tonight" from *Pocket Book of Prayer* by M. Basil Pennington. Copyright © 1986, Cistercian Abbey of Spencer, Inc. Used by permission of Doubleday, a division of Bantam Doubleday Dell Publishing Group, Inc.

"The Sacred Three" from *Every Earthly Blessing*. Copyright © 1991, Esther deWaal. Published by Servant Publications, Box 8617, Ann Arbor, Michigan 48107. Used with permission.

"Come, Holy Spirit," "To the Blessed Virgin" and "Servant of God" from *The Oxford Book of Prayer*, George Appleton, gen. ed. Copyright © 1985, George Appleton. Published by Oxford University Press, Oxford, England. Used with permission.

"At Night" from *The HarperCollins Book of Prayers*, compiled by Robert Van de Weyer. Copyright © 1993, Robert Van de Weyer. Used by permission of HarperCollins Publishers, New York, New York.

Further books of interest from Liturgy Training Publications:

LTP's Small Prayer Books:
    Catholic Prayers: A First Book
    Grant Us Peace
    Prayers of the Sick
    Prayers of Those Who Make Music
    Keeping Advent and Christmastime
    Keeping Lent, Triduum and Eastertime
    Prayers of Those Who Mourn

For a spirit shaped by the liturgy:
    Words around the Table
    Words around the Fire
    Words around the Font
    Words That Sing

Catholic Household Blessings and Prayers   *A beautiful hardcover book with prayers for every day and for the seasons, the good times, the sad times.*

The Psalter   *The new translation of the psalms in contemporary, inclusive English. Prepared by the International Commission on English in the Liturgy.*

Psalms for Morning and Evening Prayer   *The four-week cycle of psalms and canticles arranged for morning and evening prayer, and including psalms for midday and night prayer.*

Proclaim Praise   *Daily prayer for parish meetings and for the home.*

Thank God   *Prayers of Jews and Christians together.*

Children's Daily Prayer   *An annual book with prayers for each day of the school year.*

Sunday Morning   *A beautiful book introducing young children to the Sunday liturgy of the parish.*

For more information: 1-800-933-1800